Arrive and Thrive

Published by Deidre Dattoli
First Published in 2022 in Melbourne Australia
Copyright © Deidre Dattoli
ISBN 978-0-6457572-0-0

www.deidredattoli.com

All rights reserved. No part of this publication may be reproduced, stored in a retrieval system or transmitted in any form or by any means, electronic, mechanical, photocopying, recording or otherwise, without the prior written permission of the publisher.

A JOURNAL FOR WONDERFUL YOU!

CREATED BY **DEIDRE DATTOLI**
YOUTH MENTOR

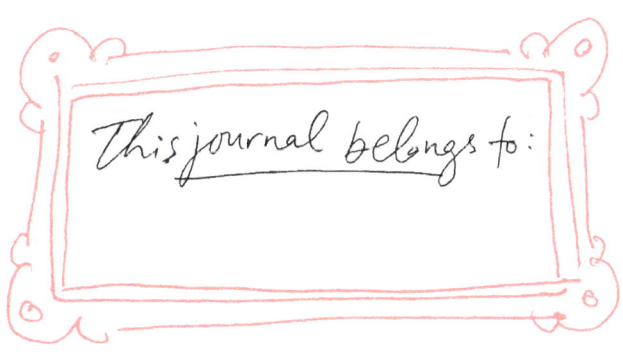

Arrive + Thrive

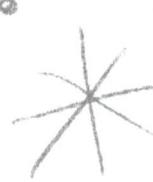

I WOULD LIKE TO THANK...

Astra Sharma, Lisa Single, Meredith Gaston and Nicki Huber-Smith, for generously giving their time and experience to the interview process; Choechoe Brereton for her guidance on and insight into the copy and her passion for my work; Richard Miller for his mad editing skills; and Kym Basoka of Inky Words for her patience and design excellence.

DEDICATION

I grew up on a cane farm in North Queensland, the second eldest of five children. It was an amazing childhood and one I'm really grateful for: open spaces to roam and explore, working on the farm and chasing bandicoots out of burning cane fields, riding horses flat out in the bush, swimming in the river and jumping off the highest rocks into its cool, inviting flow. So many great memories that, looking back, were also shadowed by a feeling of not really belonging and of never being understood because of my sensitive nature. Fast forward to my teenage years where I sought to be truly seen and to cultivate a deeper sense of who I was and why I was here. It was a voice, a surge, that grew louder and stronger. I longed to be known and for a safe place.

So began a season of discontent that regularly played out in school; I rebelled to get attention and to be seen. I acted contrary to my core values and who I really wanted to be, sparking an internal struggle that has profoundly shaped and informed my work and journey so far. Before moving in a more authentic direction, I started a hairdressing apprenticeship and made a friend who saw me for who I really was. That's when I began to explore and connect to my deeper truth.

I now have a teenage daughter, Scarlett, and this journal is dedicated to her. I wanted to create a welcoming space that helps her explore her inner world, inspires her to feel strong and connected to who she is, and backs her to follow her big, brilliant dreams. I want her to have somewhere safe to navigate the heartaches of life, and to reflect on the magic of how difficult experiences can grow and empower her. Here, she can commit to her goals and celebrate her successes.

Scarlett's childhood is a world apart from mine with very different challenges and opportunities. As a parent, I want to foster an environment in which she thrives. Through my contribution, I want the world to be a better place for her—a place she can fully express herself and feel valued for who she is and what she's achieved.

My hope is that this journal also enables you to find your value, your worth and your voice. Whoever you are, wherever you've come from, there are good things ahead. Just turn the page and take a look.

Our deepest fear is not that we are inadequate.
Our deepest fear is that we are powerful beyond measure.
It is our light not our darkness that most frightens us.
We ask ourselves, who am I to be brilliant,
gorgeous, talented and fabulous?
Actually, who are you not to be?
You are a child of God.
Your playing small does not serve the world.
There's nothing enlightened about shrinking so that other
people won't feel insecure around you.
We were born to make manifest the glory of
God that is within us.
It's not just in some of us; it's in everyone.
And as we let our own light shine,
we unconsciously give other people
permission to do the same.
As we are liberated from our own fear,
our presence automatically liberates others.

—Marianne Williamson

Arrive + Thrive

HOW DIFFERENT WOULD LIFE BE...

If you could handle the tough stuff with confidence and positivity? Y'know, with the calm strength you can't fake because it comes from a solid belief in how remarkable and capable you are. Seriously. Have you thought about it before?

Maybe you already handle your challenges well. That's pretty great. Come along for the ride anyway, you may discover something you didn't know. Maybe you don't handle your challenges as well as you would like. That's perfectly fine too.

You've probably heard the word wellbeing a fair bit or even read about it. While wellbeing can mean different things to different people, many agree that at its most basic, it means being well, which includes positive experiences such as feeling happy, healthy, socially connected and purposeful.

If you think of wellbeing as a cake, the ingredients you need to make it include self-esteem and confidence, an optimistic mindset, resilience, self-determination, motivation and positive relationships. Not only will they help you deal with challenges in ways that build your self-worth, but they'll also help you be well.

This journal is dedicated to developing the crucial ingredients for your wellbeing. It will empower you to become more self-assured and self-aware. It will build you up to be resilient and encourage you to think about things in new ways. Best of all, it will guide you to discover how truly extraordinary you are.

"Wellbeing cannot exist just in your own HEAD. Wellbeing is a combination of FEELING GOOD as well as actually having MEANING, GOOD RELATIONSHIPS and ACCOMPLISHMENT."

— Martin Seligman

Arrive + Thrive

BON VOYAGE

Work through this journal however you wish. We only suggest you read about Mindset first. Where you flip to next is up to you. Have fun and enjoy the journey of self-discovery.

MINDSET   **8**
Get the best out of yourself and any situation

SELF-ESTEEM & CONFIDENCE   **14**
Learn what makes you so darn marvellous

CULTIVATING OPTIMISM   **30**
Adjust your thinking and squash negative self-talk

RESILIENCE   **38**
Dealing with hardship and failure

DETERMINATION & MOTIVATION   **46**
Two essentials to achieving purpose

POSITIVE RELATIONSHIPS   **52**
Valuing yourself to value others

MY SECRET GARDEN   **58**
Your space to think and reflect

REFERENCES & RESOURCES   **68**
Useful info if you need a little extra support

Arrive + Thrive

MINDSET

KEEP GROWING, FLOWER!

Mindset plays a big part in getting the best out of yourself and every situation. A positive mindset helps improve every aspect of your wellbeing, from your self-esteem to your relationships.

What is mindset?

Your mindset is the ideas, beliefs and attitudes you have that shape and influence the way you think about yourself and your world. It's your mindset that determines your behaviour, your expectations in life and your attitude towards everything you go through.

"We are what we REPEATEDLY DO. EXCELLENCE, then, is not an act but a HABIT." — Will Durant

Arrive + Thrive

MINDSET

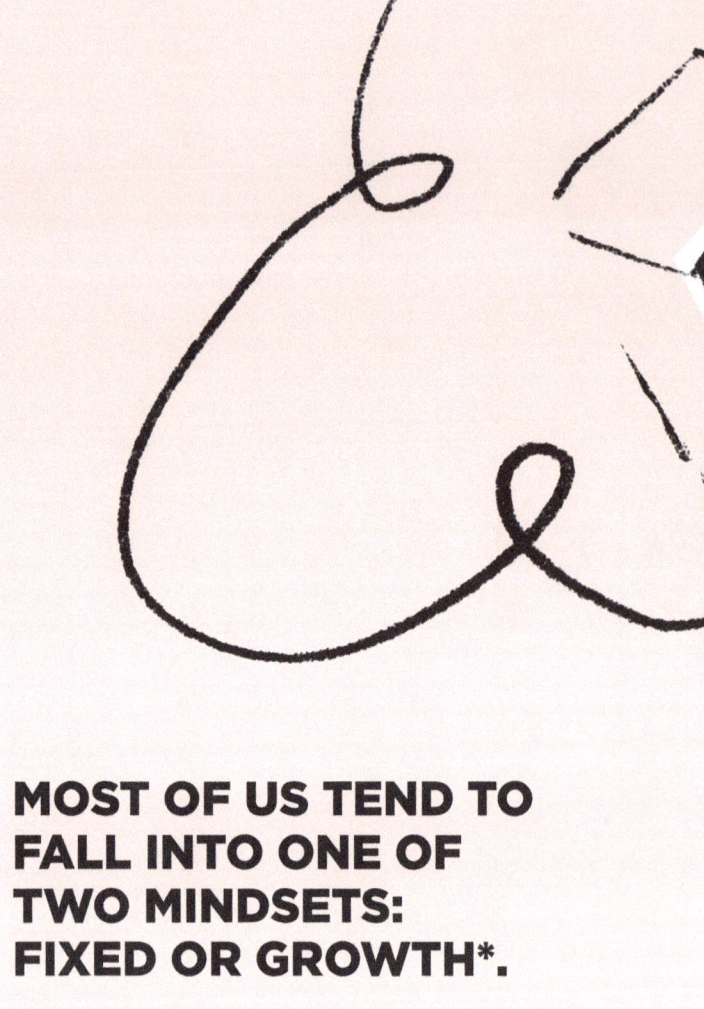

MOST OF US TEND TO FALL INTO ONE OF TWO MINDSETS: FIXED OR GROWTH*.

Fixed mindset
Someone with a fixed mindset:

- Doesn't deal well with setbacks
- Believes they have little ability
- Uses negative self-talk such as "I'll never get that right!"
- Tries to hide their mistakes
- Avoids challenges

Growth mindset
Someone with a growth mindset:

- Doesn't shy away from challenges or new things
- Learns from those around them
- Understands that to get what they want they must work hard for it
- Learns from their failures
- Knows they have weaknesses and tries to improve them

Because your mindset determines really important things, in particular, how you adapt to and deal with life, having a growth mindset empowers you to handle almost anything that comes your way. Now, if you already have a sneaking suspicion that your mindset might be a little more fixed and a little less growthy, don't stress! The good thing about mindset is that you can change it.

*Based on research by Carole Dweck

NEVER GIVE UP

Did you know that a specific part of your brain deals with routine and habit? It's called the **basal ganglia**. It's a centre for many important functions, including habits. **A habit is anything you do automatically**: cracking your knuckles, getting angry if you lose a game, or taking off your shoes by the front door when you get home. Negative self-talk and negative thinking are also habits.

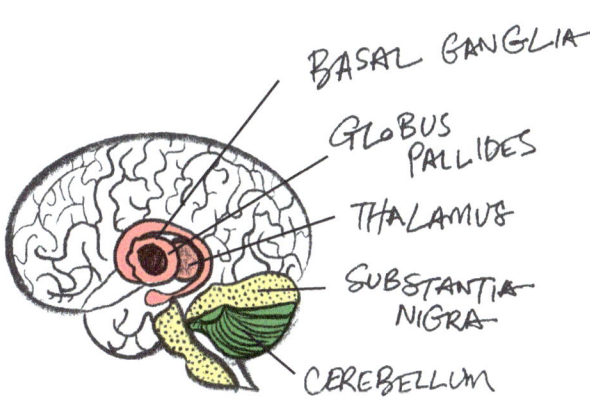

How are habits formed?

The more you perform a behaviour, the more it gets hardwired into your brain. The first time you do something a certain way, like walking to a friend's house, a connection associated with the task is formed in your brain. The first few times, you have to really concentrate to get it right; if you don't, you might take a wrong turn or get a little lost. But after walking to your friend's house the same way over and over again, the connection grows stronger until the behaviour becomes automatic. You soon realise you can get there without even thinking about it. That's how habits are formed, both **good** and **bad**.

Changing a habit

Fixed and **growth** mindsets are both a type of habit and are also achieved through repetition—thinking, acting or talking a certain way long enough for the behaviour or attitude to become second nature. Changing from a fixed mindset (negative and restricted) to a growth mindset (positive and receptive) takes time. According to science, it takes about 66 days (a little over two months) to form a new habit, which means if you want to change your behaviour, attitude and thinking to that of a growth mindset, it's really important to **keep trying and not give up.**

MINDSET

Arrive + Thrive

REFLECT ON YOUR MINDSET

Write down two or three attitudes, thoughts or beliefs that come from a fixed mindset. For each fixed attitude, thought or belief, write an alternative that reflects a growth mindset.

Fixed Mindset:

I want to be a pilot but it takes years. I'm not going to try because I won't make it.

Growth Mindset:

If it's what I really want, I'll stick with it. Especially with the support of someone who believes in me. If I loose motivation, I'll keep the goal in mind and find a way to get it back.

Arrive + Thrive

MINDSET

Fixed Mindset:

Growth Mindset:

Fixed Mindset:

Growth Mindset:

Fixed Mindset:

Growth Mindset:

Arrive + Thrive

SELF-ESTEEM & CONFIDENCE

WONDERFUL, MARVELLOUS YOU

Healthy self-esteem is built through the conscious act of valuing yourself and acknowledging your worth. As a unique entity—a prized individual and human being, born with sparkle and flare—you already have immense value and worth. Healthy self-esteem sounds a little like this: "I know I'm worthy of good things. I'm capable of creating the life I want. I deserve to have a great life." Without it, achieving all the good stuff you dream of will be difficult.

IT'S A ROCKY ROAD

Low self-esteem can be really tough. It affects your relationships and how you handle school. It can make you sensitive to what others say, and drive you to withdraw from activities and people—even those you care about. It often leads to stress, anxiety and loneliness, and can trigger serious issues such as an eating disorder, or drug and alcohol dependencies.

* If you need support for one or more of these issues, please refer to our Resources section for helpful websites and phone numbers.

Signs of low self-esteem include:

- Saying negative things and being self-critical
- Focussing on your failures and ignoring your achievements
- Thinking others are better than you
- Difficulty making friends
- Feeling unloved and unwanted
- Not accepting compliments
- Feeling sad, depressed, anxious, ashamed or angry

Low self-esteem can be caused by unsupportive parents or significant adults in your life, anxiety, bullying, loneliness, stress, bad friendships, poor body image, failing school performance, trauma, or abuse.*

Why does a healthy sense of self matter?

Healthy self-esteem will give you the courage to try new things, take considered risks and solve problems. It enables you to feel comfortable in your own skin, to better handle stress, bounce back quicker from challenges, tackle negative feelings (such as worthlessness, guilt or shame) and build happy, positive relationships. Healthy self-esteem leads to learning and development, which encourages confidence, growth and skills to shape an exciting and purposeful future. Knowing your value and worth is a key ingredient to creating a strong sense of wellbeing.

Arrive + Thrive

SELF-ESTEEM & CONFIDENCE

HOW HEALTHY IS YOUR SELF-ESTEEM?

Rate from **0 to 10** how much you believe each statement. 0 means you do not believe it at all and 10 means you completely believe it.

STATEMENT	RATINGS
1. I believe in myself	
2. I am just as valuable as other people	
3. I would rather be me than someone else	
4. I am proud of my accomplishments	
5. I feel good when I get compliments	
6. I can handle criticism	
7. I am good at solving problems	
8. I love trying new things	
9. I respect myself	
10. I like the way I look	
11. I love myself even when others reject me	
12. I know my positive qualities	
13. I focus on my successes and not my failures	
14. I am not afraid to make mistakes	
15. I am happy to be me	

TOTAL SCORE

SCORING:
0 - 50 low self-esteem; 50 - 100 satisfactory - could use some boosting; 100 - 150 healthy self-esteem

Whether you scored in the **healthy, satisfactory** or **low** range, your self-esteem always has room to grow. So how do you consciously value yourself every day? By understanding a little about what makes you deserving of your own love and respect—and that of others.

Arrive + Thrive

SELF-ESTEEM & CONFIDENCE

Think about someone you know and love, who also knows and loves you.

What is their name?

_____
_____

Why do you love them?

_____
_____

Why would you never want to hurt them or see them hurt by anyone?

_____
_____

Why do they deserve to be loved, valued and cared for?

_____
_____

If they didn't feel like they were worth anything, what would you say to encourage them?

_____
_____
_____
_____

Arrive + Thrive

SELF-ESTEEM & CONFIDENCE

NOW...
Imagine you're asking that person you know and love the same questions about yourself. What would they say? If possible, ask, text or email them these questions directly.

1. Name four reasons I should love who I am.

_____

_____

2. Why shouldn't I physically or emotionally hurt myself or allow anyone else to hurt me?

_____

_____

3. Why do I deserve to be loved, valued and cared for?

_____

_____

4. Sometimes I feel like I'm worth nothing. What am I worth to you?

_____

_____

Fill out your self-worth slip with the answers in number order. Take a picture of your slip, photocopy it or cut it out.

My name is _____ and I am _____

_____

I won't pay myself out or let anyone else bring me down because I

_____

I'm wonderful, precious and deserving of love because I

_____

Feeling worthless, ridiculous or rubbish is a thing of the past because now I know

_____

_____

ONE OF A KIND

Another great way to build value and self-worth is by knowing some of the many qualities that make you exceptional and one of a kind. Circle your best qualities, as many as you would like. If you're struggling to figure out which apply to you, take a sec to think about the positive comments trusted friends make about you.

Good Listener	Tolerant	Resourceful	Reliable
Caring	Artistic	Witty	Creative
Strong	Brave	Kind	Elegant
Sweet	A Good Friend	Hardworking	Beautiful
Confident	Outgoing	Friendly	Responsible
Thoughtful	Optimistic	Proud	Empathetic
Considerate	Patient	Generous	Organised
Energetic	Honest	Accepting	Unique
Loyal	Charming	Curious	Flexible
Positive	Intelligent	Determined	Motivated
Decisive	Adventurous	Loving	Happy
Independent	Sensitive	Real	Passionate
Calm	Open Minded	Relaxed	Caring
Proud of Yourself	Enthusiastic	Humble	Calm
Disciplined	Relaxed	Helpful	Intuitive
Enthusiastic	Adaptable	Fun	Reliable
Optimistic	Friendly	Humourous	Studious

Please list others you may think of:

_____

_____

SELF-ESTEEM & CONFIDENCE

Arrive + Thrive

What are your top three qualities?

1. I am
_____
_____

2. I am
_____
_____

3. I am
_____
_____

Whenever you feel low about yourself, read out your top three qualities. Remember: to rewire your brain you have to replace old habits with new ones, in this case, old thoughts about yourself with new, positive thoughts that are powerful and true.

Now, select three qualities you don't have but choose to work towards. Achieving new goals helps build self-esteem.

1. I will be
_____
_____

2. I will be
_____
_____

3. I will be
_____
_____

Think about ways to develop the three qualities you want. Write your ideas below:

Quality 1
_____
_____

Quality 2
_____
_____

Quality 3
_____
_____

Arrive + Thrive

SELF-ESTEEM & CONFIDENCE

DID YOU KNOW...
As many as 64% of 16-year-old girls worry about being different?*

When you understand what makes you such a brilliant human being, be it your creativity, kindness, musical talent, positivity, grace, culture, or scientific genius, you'll never want to be like anyone else again. Your uniqueness is your strength, your true source of beauty and your contribution to the world. Recognising that is an important choice you have to make. Dr Seuss puts it best when he says: "Why fit in when you are born to stand out?"

*The Worrying Trend in The Minds of Young Australian, abc.net.au

GLORIOUS CAKE & GROSS MUD

Let's talk about choice for a sec. When you choose to believe you're not worth anyone's time or attention rather than believe the truth—that you're wondrous and worth good things—it's kinda like being served with a plate of glorious cake and a plate of gross worm-riddled mud, and slurping down the squirming mud every time. Glorious or gross, your thoughts and beliefs feed your self-perception and shape you.

"But I don't choose to think badly of myself, I just do!"

Totally get it. Loving yourself can be a challenge for sure. But even allowing negative thoughts to hang around without correcting them is still choosing—to do nothing or to agree with them. Choice is a life-changing freedom. Enjoy it and make up your mind to think, know and believe you are precious.

"If you are ALWAYS trying to be normal, you'll NEVER know how AMAZING YOU CAN BE!"
—Maya Angelou

"UNIQUE + DIFFERENT is the next generation of BEAUTIFUL."
—Taylor Swift

"I can't think of any BETTER representation of BEAUTY than someone who is UNAFRAID to be HERSELF." —Emma Stone

REFLECT ON SPECTACULAR YOU

This short activity will help you get started. Answer the questions honestly and use the white space to write down anything else you think of. Be sure to include positive solutions to any negative statements.

Example statement: Something I want to change about myself is my dress size.

Positive solution: Get fit and eat well. Aim for being healthy not skinny.

Something I want to change about myself is:

Positive solution:

I've helped others by:

Compliments I have received:

I get upset when:

Positive solution:

I am happy when:

Arrive + Thrive

SELF-ESTEEM & CONFIDENCE

WELCOME TO THE SHOW!

Self-confidence means feeling sure of yourself and your ability to deal with different tasks and situations. Not in a cocky way, but with wisdom and dignity. It's a quiet assurance that says, "I can handle any situation I come across and if not, I'll figure out what to do."

When you're confident, you:

- Rarely feel insecure
- Don't shy away from challenges
- Engage in positive self-talk (refer to pg 27)
- Trust your skills and strengths to help you deal with your circumstance

A healthy level of self-confidence enables you to welcome new people, experiences and opportunities. In the wake of failure, it peps you up to try again. Low self-confidence does the opposite. It keeps you from welcoming anything new and leaves you fearful about trying again when things don't go as planned. Long-term, it causes you to miss out on the extraordinary things you can do and achieve.

Arrive + Thrive

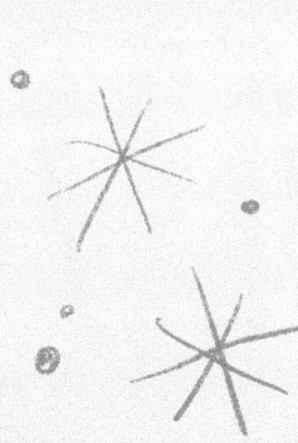

TIGHTROPES & TICKETS

If you've ever had to save for anything you'll agree that it can be slow going. Those first few dollars seem like they'll never amount to much. But little by little, the more you add, the healthier your bank balance gets until one day, you notice just how much you've accumulated.

Building confidence is very similar. Everything you do that's new, or shakes up your comfort zone, or makes you feel good, deposits a little confidence in you. Over time, you build up a healthy level.

Others (especially those you trust), add to your confidence when they tell you how clever, or kind or capable you are. But in order for their observations to make a real difference, you must believe them wholeheartedly.

DID YOU KNOW...
Young Syrian women who have fled to Turkey from their war-torn homes are being taught circus skills to help improve their self-confidence?*

Each time these sensational daredevils improve their stilt walking, tightrope crossing, or juggling abilities, their self-confidence skyrockets. They bond with their new community by making them laugh, which helps improve their sense of belonging. How impactful it is to feel good at something. It can give you the courage to face the toughest situations.

*News Deeply: Clowning Around: Refugee Women Find Confidence With Circus Skills, newsdeeply.com

Arrive + Thrive

SELF-ESTEEM & CONFIDENCE

ROLL UP! GET YOUR TICKETS HERE!

On the blank tickets, jot down up to five things you're good at. It can be anything: physics, running, swinging from a trapeze, dressage, or braiding your hair.

Whether you filled in one or all five tickets, knowing that you're good at something is half the battle won. **Take a snapshot.** These are your tickets to healthy self-confidence. When you doubt your ability to handle a new task or situation, read them and remember how capable you already are.

BE A LITTLE DARING!

There are several ways to increase your self-confidence. Listed below are some of the best, tossed in with a few fun ideas for breaking new ground.

Positive self-talk
Practise thinking that always encourages, uplifts and affirms you. (Find out how on pg. 30)

Be good to yourself
Don't take to heart any negative things others say about your abilities. Their jealousy and junky attitude is their issue. Not yours!

Growth mindset
Embrace a growth mindset to help you push through challenges and excel in phenomenal ways. (Find out how on pg. 8)

Feed your talent
Pick one of your confidence tickets to get even better at. Invest in yourself to become one of the best.

Think of an "if only" item
Identify something you've always wanted to do "if only" you had more confidence, then push yourself a little each day to do it. Paint a picture. Write a book. Build up your photography portfolio.

Take a risk
A safe one. Try out for a new sports team, take steps toward making a new friend, sign up for drama class, wear a colour you love but have always avoided, or learn a new skill.

SELF-ESTEEM & CONFIDENCE

Arrive + Thrive

NICKI HUBER-SMITH
TRAPEZE ARTIST AND ENVIRONMENTAL SCIENTIST

Page 28

I joined Aerialize when I was seven years old and have been involved in the Aerialize community for about 12 years. Circus became my main sport as the classes I took were fun and challenging. The atmosphere when training is one of the most non-judgmental of any other community I've been in.

I was never a confident child. I always joined the back of the line and never raised my hand. My lack of confidence, especially in primary school, hindered my early academic learning. It was a feedback loop of me feeling stupid and scared, not bothering with things and getting frustrated. I never learned my times tables and always thought I was terrible at maths, so in year 10 I dropped it. During my senior years of high school I realised for the first time that I actually enjoyed science. I'm now doing a Bachelor of Science majoring in Environmental Science at university. I've had to do university level physics, which has meant reteaching myself basic mathematics.

I've also been let down in quite a few friendships, and didn't realise how much it affected the way I interacted and made new friends till my late teens. I battled anxiety for most of my childhood (and more severely in my teen years), which meant I put up a wall when making friends, always being that bit too cautious to let them look through the cracks.

I still deal with this today, not really having a best friend I speak to about everything. I've never had a boyfriend either, which doesn't define who I am at all, but it does feel like my cautiousness may be noticeable to others and push anyone away before they get close. Dealing with emotions by myself all the time (especially when I have a lot of them) is hard and I often have low and better days. It's why the relief of training at Aerialize is so important to me—it allows me to be myself a bit more and not worry what others think of me all the time. I'm in Aerialize's Youth Performance Troupe, which mainly teaches acrobatics and tumbling skills. I also do a specialty in our advanced adult Static Trapeze class.

When I joined the Youth Troupe I was about 14 years old and everyone in the troupe was so talented and intimidating to me. I was very quiet and afraid to try new tricks. Now, I'm one of the oldest Youth Troupe members, have been in the troupe the longest, and often play critical roles in basing others (being the bottom lifting person).

Once I realised I'm valuable within my troupe and started to progress with my trapeze skills, I started to feel surer of myself in other aspects of life. I never used to like talking to people I didn't know and still struggle with it sometimes, but then I also think, Hey, I got that really difficult trick called "Break Your Collarbone" last week, which was way harder than this will be. It's helped me realise I'm worth being treated well, I'm worth happiness, I don't deserve to feel pressure and I deserve to feel proud of myself because, goddammit I got the "Break Your Collarbone" last week!

Being self-confident and having self-esteem has a lot to do with self-value. You may never achieve what you actually want to in life if you don't believe you can. It's the same with learning new tricks in circus: you struggle with surpassing this barrier in your brain that says you may not make it the first few times you try. And you may not—but you may. After you keep trying and get it for the first time, you know you can do it forever. Self-value is the part of the process that allows you to keep trying until you get it. It doesn't just come from achieving something, it's a course of discovering yourself, acknowledging how hard something is and trying even if there doesn't seem to be an end in sight because you're worth pushing through for what you want.

Start to notice when you hear that little voice in your head say you're bad at something. Noticing when you ridicule yourself is a serious step. Even if you can't correct how you're feeling every time, by noticing you feel this way you're halfway there. I also like to focus on things I'm proud of myself for, even if it's something as little as having a shower when I'm not feeling like it, or putting on a piece of clothing that takes me out of my comfort zone.

The positive feedback of saying to yourself, "If I can do one thing then I sure as hell can do this other thing", helps you build self-confidence in your abilities, as well as building your self-esteem by showing yourself that you're a capable person. **Self-worth doesn't come from others, it comes from the acceptance of you, by you.** Discovering who you are is a lifelong process that will never ever be over. You must accept who you are and who you want to become. **You must start to look at yourself in the present and start to love what you see, because you cannot change the past and cannot predict the future.**

CULTIVATING OPTIMISM

CHEER SQUADS & RAIN CLOUDS

Thousands of thoughts run through our heads each day. Experts say as many as 50,000 to 80,000. Luckily for those around us, we keep a large number of them to ourselves. This constant inner chatter is known as **self-talk,** and it can have a big influence on how we feel and behave.

An **optimistic mindset** (an attitude of hope and confidence about the future) starts with positive self-talk.

Arrive + Thrive

CULTIVATING OPTIMISM

Positive self-talk is like having the best inbuilt cheer squad on your side. It makes you feel good about yourself and what's happening in your life.

It sounds something like this:

- I can accomplish anything I put my mind to
- I love this challenge!
- I've got this.
- I will keep trying.
- I'm making progress.

Negative self-talk is like living under a permanent rain cloud. It gets you down even on a good day, and makes you feel terrible about yourself and your situation.

It sounds something like this:

- Why did I have to be so annoying?
- Nobody cares what I think.
- I can't do it!
- I'll always get it wrong.
- I'm not good enough, smart enough, pretty enough.

Arrive + Thrive

CULTIVATING OPTIMISM

What does your self-talk sound like?

On a scale of 1 to 5, with 1 being you don't agree and 5 being you strongly agree, score yourself.

1. You generally say negative things about yourself.

1   2   3   4   5

2. You have a hard time finding positive things in most situations.

1   2   3   4   5

3. You think your current lifestyle will limit your success.

1   2   3   4   5

4. There's nothing exciting to look forward to in the future.

1   2   3   4   5

5. You believe you can't really change how intelligent you are.

1   2   3   4   5

---

5 to 10 - You've got a pretty positive mindset!

11 to 20 - Your thoughts and your mindset might be holding you back.

21 to 25 - Your negative thoughts really bring you down.

REWIRE YOUR BRAIN AND GIVE STINKING THINKING THE BOOT

Your default self-talk is a type of habit. Though it's largely automatic, it can be changed. It takes time and requires effort at first, like learning a new language or skill. But you can do it! The more you practise, the better you get. While a positive shift in thinking may not seem particularly mind blowing, it can affect your self-esteem and emotions, which shape your confidence, the choices you make, the opportunities you take and, ultimately, your future direction.

If your self-talk already happens to be positive, well done! Practise these tips and you'll get even better at it.

Arrive + Thrive

TIP 1:
CHALLENGE NEGATIVE SELF-TALK

Write your most common negative thoughts.

_____
_____
_____

Write how they make you feel.

_____
_____
_____

Write a positive thought for every negative.

_____
_____
_____

Write how it makes you feel.

_____
_____
_____

Remember these positive words and use them to shut up any negative self-talk that sneaks into your head. That's how you build a new habit and slowly turn stinking thinking around.

DID YOU KNOW...
Nearly 60% of girls aged 14–16 wish they could change their feelings.*

Research continues to show that people who think positively tend to be happier, more optimistic and emotionally healthier. Practising gratitude every day helps with that even more.

*The Worrying Trend in The Minds of Young Australian, abc.net.au

CULTIVATING OPTIMISM

Arrive + Thrive

TIP 2:
REFLECT ON GRATITUDE

A good way to engage in positive thinking is by taking a little time to appreciate the things in life you're grateful for. Keeping a gratitude diary will focus your thoughts on the good, the rad and the lovely.

Gratitude worksheet

Today I am grateful for...

I appreciate having the following people as friends...

Which positive qualities about yourself do you appreciate most?

When you are at home what are you the most grateful for?

"Optimism is the FAITH that leads to ACHIEVEMENT. Nothing can be done without HOPE + CONFIDENCE."
— Helen Keller

CULTIVATING OPTIMISM

Arrive + Thrive

CULTIVATING OPTIMISM

MEREDITH GASTON
ILLUSTRATOR, WELLNESS AUTHOR AND COACH

Page 36

I have always been an optimistic person and a lover of life. My father tells me that when I was born I was handed to him straight away, bouncing! That said, I consider nurturing the art of positivity to be an essential part of my daily life. If we seek to know and feel radiant positivity we must choose to think, speak and act in positive ways. Our proactivity is our superpower.

Too often we berate, judge, criticise and underestimate ourselves. If our inner voice was a friend, we might not actually want to have them around us. And yet, we are with ourselves for life, keeping ourselves company. To enjoy our lives we need to be in company that we also enjoy, which is why it's non-negotiable to practise self-kindness if we want to feel happy, healthy and fulfilled. The truth is, our inner voice should be the kindest voice we know.

I am kind and gentle with myself every day. I am compassionate and forgiving. I praise and motivate myself with positive, tender and complimentary thoughts; thoughts that make me feel good and motivate me onward. Grateful thoughts are equally as powerful as kind ones. I always tune into the reasons I have to be grateful for my life—from simple, rudimentary things to very detailed, very specific things. When I find myself in a stressful or challenging moment I reframe my mindset by focussing on gratitude. It's an instantaneous fix, and helps me to move my thoughts in more useful, positive directions.

Along with thinking kind thoughts, and speaking kindly and respectfully to myself and others, I nurture my mind, body and spirit with all manner of daily self-care rituals. This begins with meditating in the morning, stretching, and starting the day gently. I make a truly nourishing breakfast full of nutrient rich, plant-based ingredients, and I take time with the way I prepare, serve and enjoy the food I create, not only for breakfast but throughout the whole day.

Choosing uplifting media, from beautiful music to great art and inspirational podcasts, also keeps me on track. I choose my media wisely, and I am always mindful about the things with which I choose to fill my mind. I actively disengage from low energy, aggressive or unkind media. We don't have a TV at home and while I use social media, I use it sparingly. I like to live in the real world, connect with nature, and be in the present moment. These are the things that make me truly happy.

Exercise keeps me feeling wonderful and I'll try anything and everything. I especially love walking, yoga, dancing, trampolining and swimming. I am very happy in my own company and have worked alone for fourteen years. That said, I love spending time with others, and make sure I am around people I feel free to be myself with—people who value positive thinking and mindful living too. This way, my relationships are joyous, mutually beneficial, healing and uplifting. Positive relationships are so important when it comes to our happiness. Wisely choosing the company we keep is a practise of self-care.

While I feel extremely healthy now and brim with energy, I have endured long periods of chronic illness in my life. This includes times throughout my childhood when I could not quite understand what was happening to me and why. I did find it hard to remain optimistic at these times, especially when feeling so extremely tired and unwell. I handled this through channelling my feelings into my journaling, documenting my experiences with words and pictures. My writings and drawings about being involuntarily tucked into bed back then became fodder for my first book *Tucked In*, later rereleased as *Your Bed Loves You*. It's extraordinary how challenges and hardships are delivered to us as opportunities for personal transformation.

More than ever our world needs our loving, positive contribution. Having an optimistic mindset allows us to thrive not only on great days but also in the face of inevitable change and challenge. When we are positive we focus on what we can do, what we can be, and what we already have to be grateful for, not to mention what we already have to feel proud of. In this way, our positivity generates energy for life, boosting our self-confidence and allowing us to experience more happiness and relaxation. With a positive mindset we actively create more beautiful, enjoyable lives. Nurturing an optimistic mindset allows us to grow more resilient and proactive in our days, translating our passions and dreams into realities, and lighting up the world.

Stay true to yourself. Respect and celebrate your individuality as a matter of priority, and be courageous, wild and free in pursuing your innermost dreams. In the words of Ralph Waldo Emerson, "To be yourself in a world that is constantly trying to make you something else is the greatest accomplishment." I also love Maya Angelou's definition of success as, "liking yourself, liking what you do and liking how you do it." It was Oscar Wilde who wrote, "Be Yourself, everyone else is already taken."

Arrive + Thrive

RESILIENCE

MADE TO LAST

What is resilience?

The ability to "bounce back" when bad stuff happens in life—and it does, to everyone. Being resilient is crucial to creating the future you want and coping with the problems you'll face along the way. It can help you deal with:

- Sickness
- Starting at a new school
- Staying on top of study and exams
- Family changes like separation, divorce or a blended family
- Losing friends and trying to make new ones
- Issues in your family
- Losing someone you love

HONOUR ROLL OF RESILIENCE

After something sad, bad or unexpected brings you down, your ability to get back up, dust yourself off and keep going is the measure of your resilience. **Resilience is not ignoring the hurt, it's choosing not to be defined by it.**

Two of the most common things you have to be resilient against are hardship and failure. Nearly everyone has encountered these twin pests, even seemingly successful people. You may have heard of these guys.

J K Rowling
AUTHOR

At 25, J K Rowling lost her mother to multiple sclerosis. She later suffered a tragic miscarriage, was divorced after 13 months of marriage, lived in a cramped apartment in Scotland, had no job or money, and was rejected 12 times by publishers. She says: "Failure gave me an inner security that I had never attained by passing examinations. Failure taught me things about myself that I could have learned no other way. I discovered that I had a strong will, and more discipline than I had suspected; I also found out that I had friends whose value was truly above rubies."

Emma Stone
ACTRESS

Emma Stone spent three years auditioning for roles without ever landing anything big. She knows how awful failure can feel and says: "Nothing really worked out ... So I think, yeah, facing rejection day after day can be really, really tough ... It is funny how the things that happen in your life can feel terrible in the moment but lead you to those [successful] places." *teenvogue.com*

Serena Williams
TENNIS CHAMPION

Though Serena Williams has 23 Grand Slam singles titles, it hasn't been a smooth ride. She lost eight major games, almost died in childbirth and ended up bedridden for six weeks. She still faces a great deal of racism. She says: "With a defeat, when you lose, you get up, you make it better, you try again. That's what I do in life, when I get down, when I get sick, I don't want to just stop. I keep going and I try to do more. Everyone always says never give up but you really have to take that to heart and really do never give up."

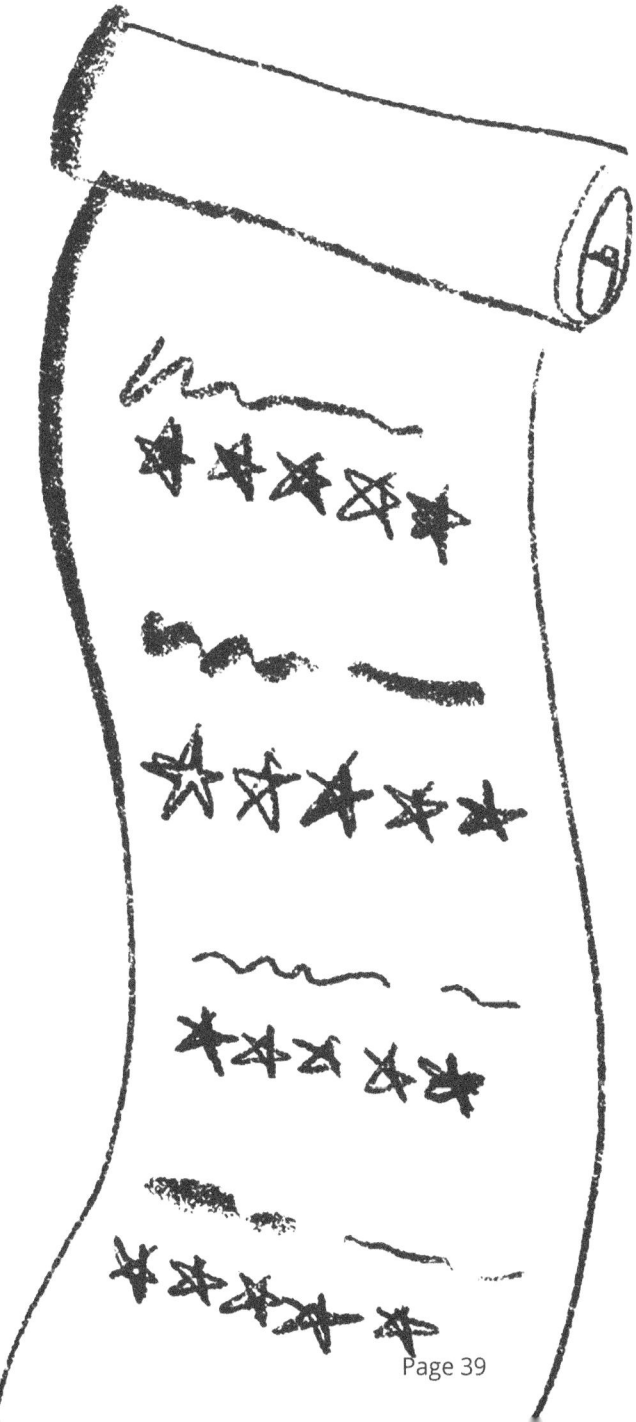

RESILIENCE

Arrive + Thrive

STAYING STRONG

Some of the factors that make you more resilient include:

- Positive thinking
- Staying optimistic
- Regulating emotions
- Learning from your failures

If you've read the previous chapter, you already know what **positive thinking** is and how it helps you stay **optimistic**. Keeping your emotions in check, like staying positive, also comes with practise.

Regulating emotions
Recognising and understanding your emotions—why you feel anxious, frustrated, confused or cranky—is important. You improve resilience when you become comfortable with how you feel and find ways to safely and appropriately express emotion (such as talking to someone you trust, giving yourself time to calm down etc.) without hurting yourself or anyone else.

Learning from your failures
Remember your **growth mindset** and all the great things it can help you do? Well, learning from your failures is definitely one of them. Instead of seeing failure as the end, a growth mindset sees it as a new beginning or an opportunity to do better. It says, "I'm not giving up, so how can I learn and improve from this setback?"

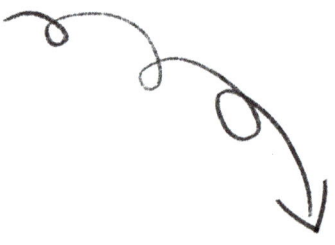

DID YOU KNOW...
The biggest worry among 14—16 year olds is their futures?*

Developing **resilience** will go a long way to helping you shape the future you want. It takes courage, perseverance, optimism and self-belief. You can do it. Just keep going and never give up!

*The Worrying Trend in The Minds of Young Australian, abc.net.au

Arrive + Thrive

RESILIENCE

REFLECT ON RESILIENCE

Write down the three biggest challenges you are facing right now.

_____
_____
_____

Write down ways to stay positive through them and how you will keep going until they're over.

_____
_____
_____

Write down the three biggest changes you want for your future.

_____
_____
_____

Write down things you can do now to start working towards them and how you're going to stay positive and keep going through hardships and failures.

_____
_____
_____

Arrive + Thrive

RESILIENCE

DRAW IT OUT

Use your creativity to design your favourite quote from the list below or choose one of your own. Remind yourself of it whenever you worry about overcoming your situation or reaching your goals.

1. **Many of life's failures are people who did not realise how close they were to success when they gave up.** — Thomas Edison

2. **It always seems impossible, until it's done.** — Nelson Mandela

3. **When someone tells you that you can't, turn around and say watch me!** — Anon

4. **Perseverance is failing 19 times and succeeding the 20th.** — Julie Andrews

5. **The sky is not my limit ... I am.** — T.F. Hodge

6. **When you get into a tight place, and everything goes against you till it seems as though you could not hold on a minute longer, never give up then, for that's just the place and time that the tide will turn.** — Harriet Beecher Stowe

7. **If you can't fly, then run; if you can't run, then walk; if you can't walk, then crawl; but whatever you do, you have to keep moving forward.** — Martin Luther King, Jr.

8. **Courage doesn't always roar. Sometimes it's the quiet voice at the end of the day whispering I will try again tomorrow.** — Mary Anne Radmacher

9. **There is no substitute for hard work. Never give up. Never stop believing. Never stop fighting.** — Hope Hicks

10. **Our greatest weakness lies in giving up. The most certain way to succeed is always to try just one more time.** — Thomas Edison

11. **Never stop dreaming, never stop believing, never give up, never stop trying, and never stop learning.** — Roy T. Bennett

12. **I will either find a way, or make one!** — Hannibal, military commander

13. **It's okay to be scared. Being scared means you're about to do something really, really brave.** — Mandy Hale

14. **Don't be pushed around by the fears in your mind. Be led by the dreams in your heart.** — Roy T. Bennett

Arrive + Thrive

Arrive + Thrive

RESILIENCE

LISA SINGLE
PILOT

Page 44

Arrive + Thrive

I first decided I wanted to fly when I was about 15 years old. I have two uncles who fly: one has his glider pilot's licence and the other his private pilot's licence. We didn't spend much time talking about flying, or about making a career of it, but they owned a Cessna 172 together and I guess in a way it normalised general aviation for me.

I found the challenge of flying very appealing. Even before my first trial introductory flight and before starting to study for my Basic Aeronautical Knowledge exam, I knew it would be a challenge and wouldn't be handed to me. I chose flying because it was different, it was exciting and I liked the potential a career in aviation would give me to travel.

I'm endorsed to fly the Cessna 150/152, Cessna 172, Cessna 206, Piper Cherokee PA-28, and the Grumman Tiger AA-5. It would be a dream come true to fly for Qantas one day. Any wide-body aircraft in Qantas' fleet greatly appeals to me. I've always had a soft spot for Boeing, so perhaps I will get to fly the Boeing 787, or arguably, the matriarch of the fleet, the Boeing 747. Who knows, but the sky is certainly not the limit.

Along with all of the wonderful things to love about flying, I've also faced some enormous challenges. When starting out, I struggled greatly with the constant mental strain my lectures and flying lessons would induce. I quickly realised that's just the way it has to be when you try to complete such a complex certification in such a short timeframe. It had a big impact on me which truly taught me how to be a motivated and driven person. That didn't happen overnight. It took a long time. Nothing was easy for me and success felt so difficult to achieve, but I got there. The challenges of time management, failure in exams or flight tests, knowing and finding true determination, disconnecting from instructors or class mates—it was all there.

Resilience is paramount, yet it's a tricky character trait to attain if you aren't naturally quick to recover from slip-ups. I think it's important to try and remind yourself that failure and hardship is not personal. You can make changes to switch the outcome from a negative one to a positive one, but it's going to require some work. I failed a few exams on my first attempt and it made me feel so lousy. As a late teen I already felt so accomplished in areas of my life, but study never came easy. I would be miserable for days after an exam and it would give me a bad attitude towards most areas of my studies. But one day, near the end of my course, I had a lightbulb moment which highlighted that failures in life are going to happen sometimes, and I could either mope and become consumed with self-pity, or I could take the feedback, accept it, learn from it and just do a whole lot better the second (or third) time round. I guess I can feel proud that giving up never felt like an option, but I had to give myself a lot of pep talks to open up the text books and just keep pushing. All of these experiences have moulded me into a very resilient person.

I look towards the end goal. It's easier than thinking about all the phases to overcome before I reach my career pinnacle. It's like hiking up a mountain: I prefer to visualise the summit rather than focus on all the steps along the way. Don't get me wrong, the journey is a wonderful, exciting part of my life which will largely be what my working life is all about, but I have a clear image of what I want to do and how I can get there, so I guess I just replay that over and over and it drives me onward and upward. **Giving up is actually not the easier option! It can seem like it, but if you give up, then you have to start again at the beginning somewhere else.** You should remember why you started in the first place, and wholeheartedly focus on that because there will absolutely be moments when giving up feels like the easier choice.

Arrive + Thrive

DETERMINATION & MOTIVATION

HOT AIR BALLOONS & ICE CREAM

Determination and motivation are a power pair for getting stuff done. Your **determination feeds your motivation** and is an intrinsic force fuelled by **purpose** (the thing or things you want to achieve).

When you're **determined** it means you've reached a decision about something and won't allow anyone or any difficulties to stop you. When you're **motivated**, it means you have a strong desire to do well or succeed at the decision you've made.

If **motivation** is a hot air balloon, then **determination** is the flame that keeps it airborne.

SO...

Purpose feels like this: I want to help the homeless by selling enough ice creams to build a homeless shelter.

Determination sounds like this: I've made up my mind to open an ice cream store one day and no one will stop me!

Motivation acts like this: Studying the craft. Perfecting your skills. Trying ice cream recipes and making mostly dud flavours. Asking for help. Never giving up until you create a range of frozen taste sensations.

DETERMINATION

Arrive + Thrive

DETERMINATION & MOTIVATION

"COURAGE, SACRIFICE, DETERMINATION, COMMITMENT, TOUGHNESS, HEART, TALENT, GUTS. That's what little GIRLS are made of.

— Bethany Hamilton

GO TO YOUR HAPPY PLACE

The best thing to do when you feel sapped or deflated is to stop and take a breather. Think about what revitalises you, then go and do it! It may be archery, whipping up macarons or listening to music in the dark. When you regularly engage in relaxing activities, you refuel to take on the next challenge.

Think about three things that restore you physically and mentally

Write them in this self-care heart with the most restorative in the No.1 spot at the top. When you need a super chilled day to replenish yourself, make it your go-to activity.

Arrive + Thrive

REFLECT ON PURPOSE & MOTIVATION

Small life purpose

What are you determined to achieve over the next week?

List possible challenges:

How will you stay motivated?

Big life purpose

Name one thing you are determined to achieve in life.

List possible challenges:

How will you stay motivated?

DETERMINATION & MOTIVATION

DETERMINATION & MOTIVATION

ASTRA SHARMA
PROFESSIONAL TENNIS PLAYER

Arrive + Thrive

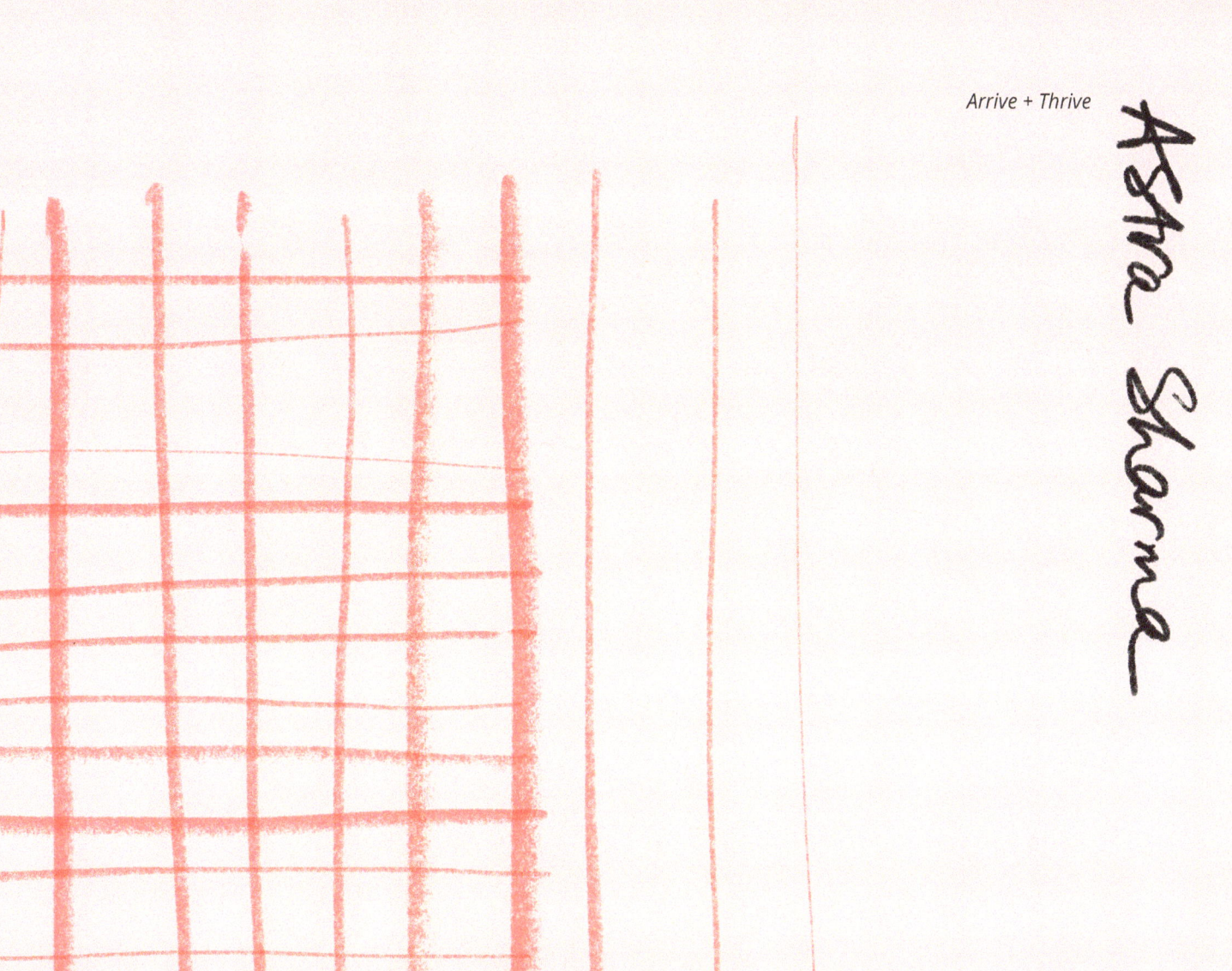

Asha Sharma

I decided to play tennis professionally at around 16 years of age, which was pretty late. I've loved the competition and competing at the highest level. The feeling of improvement and watching myself grow and move to the next level has been exciting. But I've also experienced plenty of hardship and failure; there are probably more setbacks in professional tennis than victories. There have been periods when I've had super low confidence and gone on losing streaks. Having to dig myself out of those is always a challenge. Determination and motivation plays a huge role in overcoming it all. If you don't love what you're doing you're not going to get far, or it'd be very difficult. I've always been very motivated—not by my parents or coaches, but because I've wanted to win or get better.

Determination and motivation have been defining characteristics because I started later than most in tennis. This put me at a disadvantage in terms of training and experience, but I stuck with it because it meant a lot to me and I wanted to see how good I could get. The feeling of mastering a skill definitely served as a big motivational factor. **When I lose motivation or determination, I try to talk to the people I'm closest to. I get into a dialogue about why I'm feeling the way I do.** Usually, having a reassuring voice sparks that positive motion again.

POSITIVE RELATIONSHIPS

Arrive + Thrive

SOUL FOOD

Good friends are like scrumptious food: soul nourishing and impossible to get enough of. They pick you up when you're miserable, help you out when you feel stuck and, if they're *really* good, tell you the truth when no one else will. Their quality always trumps their quantity. To identify a good friend (and to be one) it helps to understand your **values** and **self-worth**.

VALUES

Values reflect what you care most about deep down. They shape your character and what you stand for. They determine what you see as right and wrong, and how you judge good and bad. Your values drive you toward or away from different experiences and influence your behaviour. They're also responsible for how you treat others. Good friends will always respect your values (as you must always respect theirs) with one exception: if your values are destructive to you or anyone else.

MY VALUES

Step 1

Take a little time to select 10 values from the list below. Make sure they are the **most** important ones to you.

Step 2

Now you've identified 10 values, imagine you're only permitted five. Which five would you give up? Cross them off.

1. Now imagine you are only permitted four. Which would you give up? Cross it off.
2. Now cross off another to bring the list down to three.
3. And one more to bring it down to two.
4. Finally, cross off one of your two values. Which remaining value do you care about most?

Achievement	**Economic security**	**Intuition**	**Quality relationships**
Advancement	**Effectiveness**	**Involvement**	**Quality of what I do**
Adventure	**Exercise**	**Job tranquility**	**Recognition (respect)**
Affection	**Family**	**Joy**	**Religion**
Arts	**Financial**	**Knowledge**	**Reputation**
Challenging problems	**Freedom**	**Leadership**	**Responsibility**
Change and variety	**Friendship**	**Learning**	**Accountabilty**
Close relationships	**Growth**	**Location**	**Security**
Community	**Having a family**	**Loyalty**	**Self-respect**
Competence	**Helping other people**	**Making a difference**	**Serenity**
Competition	**Helping society**	**Meaning**	**Sophistication**
Cooperation	**Honesty**	**Nutrition**	**Spirituality**
Country	**Independence**	**Physical challenge**	**Stability**
Creativity	**Influencing others**	**Power and authority**	**Status**
Decisiveness	**Inner harmony**	**Privacy**	**Supervising others**
Democracy	**Integrity**	**Public service**	**Trust**
Ecological awareness	**Intellectual status**	**Purity**	**Vitality**

POSITIVE RELATION

Step 3

Take a look at the top three values on your list.

1. What do they mean to you?

   _____
   _____
   _____

2. How will you uphold them?

   _____
   _____
   _____

3. How would you like your friends to uphold them?

   _____
   _____
   _____

4. Which friends respect your values?

   _____
   _____
   _____

5. Which friends don't respect your values?

   _____
   _____
   _____

6. How will you respect your friends' values?

   _____
   _____
   _____

Arrive & Thrive

POSITIVE RELATIONSHIPS

ROCK YOUR CROWN

Self-worth

It's been said that others learn how to treat you based on **what you accept from them.** This is particularly true in friendships and relationships. Understanding your worth—how precious, wondrous and irreplaceable you are—will go a long way to deciding what you will or will not tolerate. Self-worth determines your level of self-love and self-care. It's impossible to despise something you cherish.

Famous poet, Maya Angelou, saw self-worth as a beautiful statement piece. She said, "Your crown has been bought and paid for. Put it on your head and wear it." Though you may be tempted to hide your value or tell yourself it doesn't exist—don't! You are truly more precious than rubies.

Boundaries

Believe it or not, boundaries are extremely healthy and help you care for yourself and others. "No" is one of the most difficult words girls (and women) struggle to say. We want to please everyone, even if that means ignoring our own needs. What that amounts to is a dangerous sense of responsibility.

IMAGINE

It's Friday night and you've had an intense week. You're exhausted. All you want to do is slip into your pyjamas and watch a good movie. Then your phone rings. It's your best friend. She's just heard about an amazing party and wants you to join her. "It'll be the party of the month," she insists. "Everyone will be there!" You don't want to go but you don't want to let her down or miss out either.

What do you do?

_____

_____

_____

_____

Save your friendships and your sanity

In simple terms, a boundary is the answer to the question: **What is the most self-loving thing to do in this moment?** Initially, it may seem uncaring to say **"no"** to a friend, but in actual fact it's caring on two levels.

1. You care for yourself by making the choice that upholds your worth and values, and restores your strength, energy and sanity.

2. Though your friend may not know it at the time, you're saving her from your resentment at being dragged out, your crankiness from being tired, and her guilt that it's her fault you're somewhere you don't want to be. Everyone may talk about the party at school on Monday, but you know your status and confidence doesn't come from doing what everyone else does. It comes from knowing who you are and what matters to you most.

How saying "no" upholds your worth and values

Let's say one of your values is integrity. To say "yes" to a friend when you actually want to say "no" wouldn't be in keeping with being honest and upstanding. Perhaps you value reputation. Would you rather be known as someone whose word can be trusted, or someone who says one thing and means or does another? If your decision gives you permission to do something you really need, then it's an act of self-love and self-care. See how it all works?

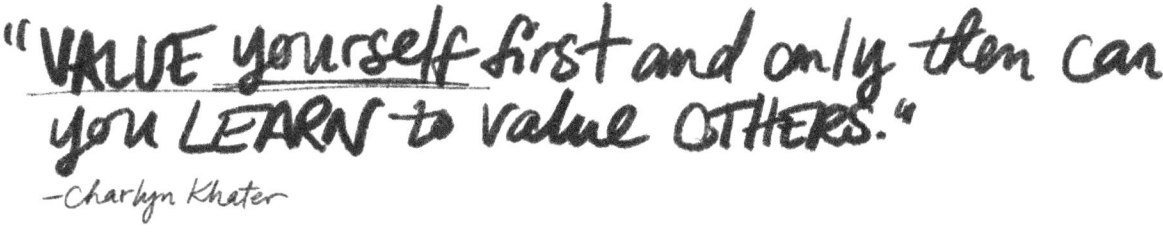

"VALUE yourself first and only then can you LEARN to value OTHERS."
—Charlyn Khater

Arrive + Thrive

POSITIVE RELATIONSHIPS

REFLECT ON SELF-LOVE

Think about times when saying "no" has been difficult. Then think about what the most self-loving thing to do in that moment would have been. Write how it's a positive decision for you and for the other person involved.

1.

It's difficult to say no when

The most self-loving thing to do would be

It's a good decision for me because

It's a good decision for my   [insert person e.g. friend, dad, mum, brother, sister, boyfriend]

because

2.

It's difficult to say no when

The most self-loving thing to do would be

It's a good decision for me because

It's a good decision for my   [insert person e.g. friend, dad, mum, brother, sister, boyfriend]

because

3.

It's difficult to say no when

The most self-loving thing to do would be

It's a good decision for me because

It's a good decision for my   [insert person e.g. friend, dad, mum, brother, sister, boyfriend]

because

Arrive + Thrive

MY SECRET GARDEN

This is your space to mentally meander, reflect and dream big about what comes next. To help are some nifty prompts that encourage you to think about things—all the new things you want to sow, nurture and grow.

SOW

What have I learned?

In what way has this journal encouraged me?

What changes will I make today?

What am I feeling?

What will I do to help or improve how I feel?

How do I want to think about myself from now on?

How will I let others treat me?

What do I want my future to look like?

What dream am I motivated to make a reality?

Why do I believe I can achieve what I set out to do?

WATER

How will I stick to any change I make?

How will I stay positive about who I am?

It matters most to me to

I want to improve in

Who will I talk to if I need encouragement?

How will I achieve any dream I want to make a reality?

What do I hope to achieve by pursuing my dream?

Who can I ask if I need help or support?

What's my plan for staying motivated?

GROW

What does success look like to me?

What could prevent me from achieving success?

What are two possible reasons that would make me give up?

How will I deal with wanting to quit?

How will I deal with failure along the way?

How will I use what I've learned through this journal in everyday life?

Why will I never ever give up on myself no matter what I face?

Am I really determined to make changes?

Okay then, starting today, I will

As a wonderful, capable and valuable human being, I can

One last thing I want to say to myself

Arrive + Thrive

NOODLE NOOK

Take a little time to relax and dream big about who you want to become and what you want to achieve in life. Big means BIG. If you could do anything what would it be? Write down your thoughts. Circle the ones you're particularly passionate about. If you can think of anything that might be holding you back from achieving what you want, write it down and include possible ways to tackle it.

Arrive + Thrive

CELEBRATE

After all this self-reflection a little self-celebration is in order. Celebrating you is super important: who you are, what you have achieved so far, how incredibly funny, or clever or talented you are, something good you've done publicly or privately. Write down everything awesome about you and all the things others admire about you too. Take a snapshot. This is a keeper!

Arrive + Thrive

BETTER TOGETHER

So many incredible things can be achieved with the help of others. We all need just one person who will pick us up, cheer us on and refuse to let us quit. If you can think of such a person (and you honestly just need one), think about how you want them to support you. Then, fill out this invitation and send it to them in a text or email.

AN INVITATION TO ADVENTURE

I _____ invite you **INSERT PERSON'S NAME** _____ to walk beside me

in this amazing, scary, crazy adventure called life. When I thought of who I wanted to support me most,

I thought of you.

I want to ask you to cheer me on when I'm _____, cheer me up when

I'm _____, keep me grounded when I'm _____,

help me stay focussed when I'm _____ refuse to let me quit when I'm

_____ and tell me the truth when I'm _____.

This invitation is my promise to let you be a positive influence in my life. Every Holmes needs a Watson. Think about it and let me know.

NOTES

Arrive + Thrive

Arrive + Thrive

NOTES

NOTES

Arrive + Thrive

Arrive + Thrive

NOTES

USEFUL CONTACTS

If you need someone outside of family and friends to talk to about any issue that's getting you down, here are some useful websites and numbers:

Lifeline
lifeline.org.au | 13 11 14

Kids Helpline (for ages 5 to 25)
kidshelpline.com.au | 1800 55 1800

Suicide Call Back Service (ages 15+)
suicidecallbackservice.org.au | 1300 659 467

SOURCES

The Worrying Trend in The Minds of Young Australian
abc.net.au

Forbes forbes.com

Health Direct healthdirect.gov.au

Medium medium.com

Positive Psychology News positivepsychologynews.com

Psychology Today psychologytoday.com

ReachOut au.reachout.com

www.ingramcontent.com/pod-product-compliance
Lightning Source LLC
Chambersburg PA
CBHW041713290426
44109CB00029B/2862